I0075110

The CFO Who Quit Her 6 Figure Job to Chase Her Dreams, Paige Burkes

by Ben Gothard,

Founder & CEO of Gothard Enterprises LLC

Author of CEO at 20: A Little Book for Big Dreams

Text and Illustration Copyright © 2017 by
Benjamin Pressner Gothard. All rights reserved.

All rights reserved. This book or parts thereof
may not be reproduced in any form, stored in
any retrieval system, or transmitted in any form
by any means — electronic, mechanical,
photocopy, recording, or otherwise — without
prior written permission of the publisher, except
as provided by United States of America
copyright law. For permission requests, contact
the publisher at:

bgothard@gothardenterprises.com

ISBN: 1946941050

ISBN-13: 978-1946941053

Project EGG
ENTREPRENEURS GATHERING FOR GROWTH

Project EGG is an elite network of entrepreneurs, authors & incredible people who problem solve, bounce ideas off of each other, share their stories and succeed together.

This mastermind includes people from around the world who are making a difference right now. We have a truly incredible group of people, like CEOs, CFOs, founders, national best-selling authors, inventors, marketers, coaches, consultants, musicians, speakers, and many many more entrepreneurs from every corner of the globe.

In the official Project EGG podcast, hosted by myself, Ben Gothard, different members of the group are interviewed. Each interview is a deep-dive into the life of the guest as both the guest and I drill down into entrepreneurship and personal development. By sharing their life and experiences, we can all learn something valuable.

This book is a transcription of the interview, unedited. Hopefully you can get as much out of the interview as I did hosting it!

Ben: Hey everybody, thanks for listening today. I'm here with Paige Burkes from Metairie, Louisiana. That's actually where I grew up from so this is a pretty special interview. Paige, you want to introduce yourself?

Paige: I am Paige Burkes; yes I grew up in Metairie outside of New Orleans. I went to school in Boston. I started my career there and now I'm out in beautiful Colorado where I've been for about twenty years.

Ben: Fantastic. Alright, well let's jump right into it. So the first question I have for you today is: what is your story?

Paige: My story. How much time do we have?

Ben: As much as you'd like.

Paige: Growing up through high school. I tried to be the best student I could. Did what everybody said you're supposed to do—graduated with honors and all that. I went to Boston College where at first I had no idea what I wanted to do but decided that Accounting seemed fun. I know that might be very strange. So I was an Accounting major there, did really well in school and I felt like I was—ever since my earlier days in high school, I did what everybody was supposed to do. You go through school, you get good grades, you go to a good college, you get a good job, you stay at your job, climb the ladder, get married, have your two and a half kids and a white picket fence. I followed along that path.

Started a career with a big public accounting firm in Boston, was trying to make partner faster than anybody, and all of a sudden I started to get this feeling of wow, is this really what I want to do the rest of my life? And the more I thought about it, the more I looked at the partners in the firm and their lives and talked to them I thought, no, this is not for me, but I had no idea what was. So I kind of took a leap and left the... call it a prestigious job with all the benefits and pay and everything, and just took off without really knowing what was next.

My husband at the time was a pilot and he was based out on the island of Nantucket so I moved out to Nantucket and basically helped a woman run a bed and breakfast and I thought, maybe that's it. I learned enough about that to say that's not what I wanted to do and just worked odd jobs on the island in the off-season. My intuition started to come to me which is I'd never been quiet enough or thought about intuition. I had my one, five, ten, twenty year plans and that was my mission. But not having those plans, my intuition started speaking up and it kept saying, go west and do something with horses. And here I was, a city girl. I didn't know anything west or horses or anything else other than we used to escape Mardi Gras and go skiing once a year but that was about it.

The logical side of me is asking that intuition, west? Where west? That's awfully big and what's with horses? What do I know about horses? I rode them in summer camp when I was a kid and it just kept saying it over and over and louder and louder so it's almost like I couldn't not listen. Since I really didn't have a plan at that time, I just told my husband, I don't know what it is but I got to go west. And he was used to me having everything all planned out and he's like what's the plan? I said, you know, for the first time there is no plan. I just remember sitting at dinner and he got all bug-eyed and he was like, what do we do? And I'm like, we just go with the flow — which was not my nature at the time.

So it was like, alright, we're leaving in two weeks and I just packed up, took a couple weeks off of work and we packed up the jeep and all I said was let's get to Colorado as fast as we can and we're just going to drive all around, all the west. Colorado, Wyoming, Montana, over to Idaho, down the west coast and my brother lived in San Francisco at the time and I said, either something's going to come up along the way or I'm going to end up at my brother's house. So after about two weeks of driving and exploring, nothing came up and we got to my brother's and were like, well now what?

My husband at the time—I say at the time because we got a divorce—he went back to Boston, went back to work, and I hung out at my brother's for a couple of weeks just trying to figure things out and did research online to figure out, okay outfitting school, that's west and horses. So being a total city girl, of course the logical thing for me to do is to go live in a tent in the middle of the woods in Jackson Hole, Wyoming and learned how to be an outfitter. So I signed up for the school and did that. And I would say it was—I'm not sure if I knew it at the time—a transformative experience. I was just so up for anything that I loved it. I just dove headfirst into whatever was the next thing to do, to discover. My intuition said west and horses and I was like, I'm in Wyoming, this is west and that has horses so let's give that one a shot.

After doing that for a month and a half, I graduated from that school and I didn't want to be an outfitter but the year before for a vacation I'd been to a dude ranch in Telluride. So I thought maybe dude ranch, that's got horses. So I managed the dude ranch for about a year and learned a whole lot there as well but thought, okay that's not quite it either. And then I worked at Colorado State University's equine program and helped with their horses and learned some things—basically learned how to train horses. Through that, I volunteered with some equine therapeutic programs that helped kids and adults with all kinds of disabilities—

basically have them, we walk with them where they ride horses and it's an incredible therapy and it can transform lives. It's pretty amazing.

So all along the way, I was trying something different and each time I feel like, okay, I learned x, y, and z about whatever the thing was and about myself, and then I would take little pieces from each step that I went through to say, this is what I did like, this is what I didn't like. Do more of what you like and less of what you don't like. So I was always trying to put the pieces together to say, okay, what am I piecing together here? So I actually met my now husband when I was managing the dude ranch. He managed the wildlife center. About the time I was leaving the dude ranch, the owner of the wildlife center was shutting the place down and my husband ended up taking the three mountain lions they had there which, long story short, we've had mountain lions for the last twenty years on our property.

We were trying to find our way; we managed a couple of horse ranches and did some other things. I basically got to the point where I was tired of making minimum wage, either taking care of other people's horses on their property. I thought, you know, I want my place, I want my horses, I'll go back to doing what I do well which is the finance thing so we can afford to have our own ranch, our own horses. So that's what I did and I got a job as a CFO in Colorado Springs and we bought our twenty acres about an hour and a half outside of Colorado Springs—it's kind of up in the woods in the middle of nowhere—and got our horses and our beautiful house.

Since then, we've had three kids and lived what I'd say is a bit of an alternative lifestyle but very much in line with our values. Living very intentionally, setting things up, kind of creating our own lives the way we wanted instead of what society or anybody expects of us. A lot of times I can work from home and a lot of people are like, how does a CFO work from home? And I'm like, well, you figure it out if that's the way you want it to happen; you kind of make things work.

So that's what I've been doing, essentially for about almost the last twenty years. We still live in the same place in the middle of nowhere which we love. When people come out to see us they're just like, man, you guys are out there. But we wouldn't have it any other way. We stood on the front porch and have this beautiful view of Pikes Peak and having managed the dude ranch, I say all the time, we'll be sitting on the front porch having coffee in the morning and I'm like, do you know how many thousands of dollars people pay to come to a place like this, to sip their coffee and look at this view for one week, and then they go back to their crazy lives and we get to do this 24/7, anyday.

Ben: That's incredible. That's an amazing story and thanks for sharing that, but I do have a few questions. When you were saying a lot of people follow, or at least advise to follow the same routine of going to school, get good grades, get into a good college, get a good job, climb the corporate ladder and then have this white picket fence. Do you think that that is the ideal situation for everybody or what would you suggest to kind of breakaway from that? How would you break away from that?

Paige: I mean, that could be the perfectly good thing for some people. I think there are a lot of people following that who are very unhappy because it's almost ingrained in us. You just do what you're supposed to do and don't ask questions, and that's what I did for quite a while. It's when you take the time to ask yourself the questions. To me, the guiding principles in anybody's life should be your core values. What are your three core values? It's who you are, what you're about, the three most important things to you that won't change through your life. You can get online and look up example lists of values and I think it's an important exercise to go through. To get to a value, like what is truly a value? Things like family or what a lot of people say and would certainly initially on my list.

But I went through a program with somebody who said values are the things you get to if you can ask the question — if you think money is a value, you have to ask, what does that get you? What feeling does that create? Well money gets you something or family creates happiness in relationships and if you can ask what does happiness get you? And happiness just gets you happiness. When you get to the end of that line of questioning of what does that get you, you've reached a value. Health, happiness, integrity — there's a million — sometimes humor. It's different for everyone, but if you can get very crystal clear on what your top three values are, base every decision in your life around those values and you can't go wrong.

So if you work for a company whose values are different than yours, you're never going to be happy there. On that note, I had a job offer from a candy company and I looked at the ingredients in their candy and I'm like a super duper health nut. I looked at the ingredients in their candy and it was red dye #6, yellow dye this, high fructose corn syrup, and all these really nasty ingredients and I was like, when they called me for the job and I'm like, I can't work for the poison company; total clash in values. But if it were like where I work now, I have a blog on mindfulness. I help people use mindfulness in sort of seeing things in a different light, to be happier. Right now, I'm the CFO of a community behavioral health company that helps people with therapy or whatever it takes for them to be happier. What we do here as a business is very much in line with what I personally want to do in the world so it works.

Ben: So when you were saying a little bit earlier in the interview how you left this job that you've spent a lot of time getting with your big accounting firm, can you just kind of describe the process of being in the moment and just leaving, just getting up and going? I mean, were you scared, were you excited? Because I think that a lot of people struggled to make that jump. Maybe you could give some advice to people who are about to start on their own journey.

Paige: I guess if you ask yourself the question, if I keep doing the same thing over and over and not making a change, what will my life be like in two, five, ten, twenty years? What kinds of regret will there be and how happy am I going to be along the way? It can be scary but quite honestly, I never felt scared. It was more like if I don't do it now, when am I going to do it? And I can always come back in that particular job for the public accounting firm. It's an international firm basically, if I ever wanted to go back, I could probably get a job with them. I had a pretty good reputation there so if everything came crashing down I can just go back.

Knowing that, and it's like even if they didn't take me back, it's not like I'm not going to go be homeless or something. I did not have some giant savings account to live on. In hindsight, I called it a two-year sabbatical. I did not have a bunch of money in the bank to just burn through for two years. I had no idea where I was going, no idea how long I'd be wherever I was going. Every step along the way I was basically just working but I found a job that was in alignment—back then, it was west and horses—as long as it fit that criteria, because my intuition said that's what I was supposed to do at the time, I was open for it.

I was at one point making 7.25 an hour feeding horses and scooping out stalls, but I was like, well, the guy that manages this place can help me to learn how to train horses and who knows where that'll go. So I never looked at anything as kind of a bad situation. I mean most of those things, I left this great firm with great pay to go get minimum wage or less for two years but it was never a problem. I remember showing up at Burger King one day and dumping out a coffee can of change to pay for some fries. I was like, that's where I am right now; I'm not going to be here forever.

Ben: That's incredible.

Paige: It was just the choices I made had me right there and well, this will change, I can't do this forever but I'm learning while I'm here.

Ben: So when you said that you really trusted your intuition, you said it took you a while — that you heard it at first, but then it eventually got so overwhelming that you just decided to listen to it and really dive right in. Do you think that you would have been successful and you would've had such a transformative experience if you had not dove 100% in?

Paige: I don't think anybody could be really successful at anything if they don't commit to it. I don't know if I looked at it that way but I was committed to whatever I created of my life up to the point of leaving that firm, I felt like every step of the way I was trying to make my parents happy, I was doing what society tells you to do, and it just hit me that, is this what I want? And the answer to that was no but there was just no answer of okay, what do I want? I don't know. I haven't experienced to have to know what I want.

The intuition, like I said, was loud enough that I couldn't avoid it, I couldn't ignore it. It would've been miserable if I had. It's like suppressing emotions, dreams, whatever. At some point, something's going to blow so I just went with it so I was committed to finding out what being open to whatever west and horses was supposed to open me up to. Ultimately, I think that's how I found my husband and all the little steps along the way were part of an evolution for me to learn about who I am and what I want out of my life and how I want to put the pieces together. Some things work, some things don't, you take what works and learn from that and keep going.

Ben: And I'm glad you kind of came back to the little pieces part because I have a question about that one. When you were saying you took all the little pieces to put together your big picture, how did you know which little pieces to keep and which to discard and say, okay, this is not for me?

Paige: Say what makes you happy and what doesn't? I like being around horses but I don't want to work for somebody else taking care of there's. I love helping with the equine therapy; it's like the feeling I get from that—am I supposed to do equine therapy specifically or am I supposed to help people in different way, something more uniquely me. And that's something I've created with the blog I have out with mindfulness. That's a different way to help people. I didn't realize, I never volunteered or anything before those experiences so I had no background. It's like, wow, I really like helping people in these certain kinds of ways and so that opened a new door for me to explore. Every little thing you do can be an opportunity to learn more about yourself. Like I said, it's pretty easy to know; does it make you happy? Does it help you? Does it make you feel good inside? Do more of that.

Ben: Right. Moving forward, what do you think is the one most important thing that you want to accomplish in your lifetime?

Paige: I don't have a bucket list; I gave that up a long time ago. I've thought about that and with years going by, accomplishments and success can't be anything that are sort of externally defined. I feel like I live day-to-day. I honestly on most days say, will I have any regrets if tomorrow's my last day on earth? And I try to live each day as sort of my own response to that. So am I doing as much as I can every day to help all the people I can given the energy that I have in a day? Even though I'm a CFO and I have my staff and everything, what I've learned in various companies I've worked for over the years is, you don't realize how much of an impact you have on the people that are just around you on a day-to-day basis.

That really hit me one time when I left the job. They're kind of giving me little going away party and this woman who—she was in sales—and I had talked to her every now and then but my Controller I think was more friends with her and I talk to my Controller a lot just on a personal level. With the little going away party, this woman in sales came up to me in tears and gave me the biggest hug and said, you will have no idea what kind of impact you had on my life. And I thought, I didn't know I had any impact on this woman's life. And I've had other people, whether it's work or otherwise, say that to me. You can just go along being you, but being you is kind of an amazing blessing to a lot of other people. Certainly not everybody, but you never know what kind of lives you'll touch.

So I would love to say, oh I want to help ten million people through my website do all this other stuff; well I don't know if I'll ever do that but I love knowing that I've helped one person. Whether that's somebody that works with me, for me, somebody who reads my blog or whatever information I've put out there. Just on a day-to-day basis, I do whatever I can to put my best out to the world and I just kind of know somewhere, somehow, it helps; and I think that's the best accomplishment. Trying to climb the highest mountain, the corporate ladder or whatever it is, I'm done with all of that. It makes me happy trying to make other people happy but I'm not hung up on their happiness. I've no control over how people respond to me. I can only control me, my thoughts, my actions, so I do the best I can every day and hope I'm doing well in the world.

Ben: It seems like your journey, you've really had to listen to yourself and really look inside for some insight but had there been any people who have really helped you along the way, sort of like mentors to you?

Paige: Early on, not so much. After my little sabbatical and we bought our house, I started to realize all the... I guess my dysfunctional thinking and ways of being created a lot of havoc in my marriage and I started to see that I was repeating patterns—negative patterns. And so I was like, you keep doing what you've always done, you get what you've always got, and I didn't know how to change myself but I thought I can't keep doing the same thing so I just need to at least choose a new response, whatever it is, and sometimes no response is a different response. Through that, I started reading all kinds of different personal development, self-development books and things online. Just learning more about how can I reprogram myself? How can I think, act, react more productively? So that I can get what I want out of life and I don't keep having these really crappy situations repeat themselves over and over.

That, all of that, what I learned and how I was able to transform my own life—which is definitely a work in process, never done—I didn't have a person in front of me, other than I'd say my husband has been an immense supporter for me and has helped me through the processes of being a good mirror for the things I want to change in myself. He's been supportive and patient and understanding throughout that process but it was how I changed my own life that led me to start my website to try to help other people do the same thing.

Ben: With your website, I'm sure you give a lot of advice to people and offer some really good insight. Could you maybe give people some more information about your website?

Paige: Sure, it's called SimpleMindfulness.com, Simple Steps to a Happier Life. When you go to the homepage, you can just put in your email and you'll get a free copy of the mindful living guide which goes through different aspects of your life—through relationships, physical health, emotional, mental, a lot of different areas and it touches on what is mindfulness and how it can help you to see the world just a little bit differently. To help you... if you see things differently, you interpret it differently, and then you act a little differently and it's a lot of little baby steps but it can add up to a much better life. I also have a program called

Mindful Body which helps you to use mindfulness to live healthier—it's not really a diet program, although I guess you could use it that way—but emotional eating, emotional responses, getting toxins and things out of your diet, out of your environment using mindfulness effectively to feel better physically. And I've been working on some other programs that are coming up as well.

Right now, I'm looking more at how to incorporate mindfulness into business. I've worked with a lot of startup companies where entrepreneurs think, oh I have to go raise ten million dollars before I can do anything and this is the only way you can start a company and you have to get this high-paid team or whatever it is, and I'm like, whoa, time out. Do you even know what kind of company you're creating? This is your company; your company is your life. Your company—do you want it to own you or do you want to own it? Because the way a lot of people start off, sort of like starting life on that path that everybody thinks you're supposed to take.

Entrepreneurs, a lot of the time, start companies on this path they think they're supposed to take. Things have changed a lot. You don't need a ton of money to start most companies. There's a ton of huge ones that started in somebody's garage and they bootstrapped them and turned them into a billion dollar companies. It's using mindfulness to say, to really think about what are you creating? Because think one, five, ten years in the future, what do you want that company to be like? What do you want the culture to be like? Because your life has to fit into that. Make decisions now, today, and every day with that vision in mind. How do you want to live every day? Do you want to be working a hundred hours a week? Well then how can you make choices today so that you can grow your company but leverage yourself, your time, technology such that you want to work forty hours but have this huge company? There are ways to do that. If you want to work a hundred hours, go for it.

But be very mindful about your decisions and you're going back to your values. What's really important to you? I mean a lot of people, they don't even know what's important so they feel like they have to run things a certain way and they pull in investors; you pull in investors, you're putting on handcuffs. Do you want that? Sometimes it may be a good thing, a lot of times it's not but people don't stop to think about that because they just think well, that's the only way to do it. I'm looking at ways to bring mindfulness to the business world; whether it's entrepreneurs and how they build companies, run companies, how people operate in their day-to-day work world as employees, consultants, anything like that.

I just think the expectations of society have gotten kind of completely out of whack and we need to bring it back to; it's like, we're all working ourselves to death. You know why? Oh, to have more money. To be happy. Well, there are ways to be happy without killing yourself. Either kind of reel it back and get to the basics.

Ben: I only have two more questions for you; I know you're really busy. If you could pass on one piece of advice, what would it be?

Paige: So it's sort of combine find your values and live by them. Be committed to living by your values.

Ben: That's great. And I guess my last question will be: is there anything about yourself that I did not ask you about today that you think is an important part of who you are that you'd like to share?

Paige: I think we've covered a lot of this. I want to turn my website into much more of a business that could really help a lot more people. But there's only enough hours in a day and my family is really important to me to. I do the best I can and say you do your best every day because that's the best you can do and every day's different.

Ben: That's phenomenal. Alright, well thank you very much for spending time here today.

Paige: Thank you.

Ben: Everybody, this is Paige Burkes from Metairie, Louisiana.

Paige: Thanks.

Ben: Bye.

www.ingramcontent.com/pod-product-compliance
Lightning Source LLC
Chambersburg PA
CBHW032021190326
41520CB00007B/578